# Women's Experience Coloring Book

## A Playful Journey in Healing and Hope

By

Nancy Scheibe

Creative Journeys Publications * Ely, MN

Published by:

 **Creative Journeys**
1764 North Highway 21
Ely, MN 55731

creativejourneys@2z.net

Cover design by Nancy Scheibe

Library of Congress Cataloging in Publication Data
Scheibe, Nancy R.
     Women's Experience Coloring Book: A Playful Journey in Healing and Hope/Nancy Scheibe;
     Illustrations by Nancy Scheibe
     p. cm.
     ISBN 0-9641524-7-9
     1. Psychology (Self-actualization). 2. Personal Development.
     3. Interpersonal Relations. 4. Workbook. I. Title.

Printed and Bound in the United States

# Dedication

I dedicate this book to my mother, Myrtle, whose loving spirit remains long after her early passing, and to my father, Roland, for his dedication to keeping our family together.

To my husband Doug, a treasured man who travels the journey with me and sprinkles my life with love and laughter.

To my children whose well being necessitated my own healing:
Wade, whose gentle soul and sparkling eyes forever inspire creativity,
Sara Jo, who mirrors me and challenges my purpose, and
Naomi, whose playful free sprit inspires my sprit onward.

And to women everywhere!

# The Contents of Life

# Acknowledgements

Many people have touched my life and left their mark, some painful, most joyful.
Each of them has contributed to who I am and I am grateful.

My family has offered unending patience and support for my growth and my work. I especially want to thank Carl and Jean Scheibe, Kris Kayser, Lisa Chronister, Glenda Huston, Deb Cohen, Deborah Dora, LouEzza Bradley, Marie Burgeson, Christine Woods Jones and Karen Bodin for their bright spirits and honest encouragement. Thank you to Sally Butler, editor extraordinaire, for her assistance with this edition. I also thank my four-legged friends Mickey, Corky and Ty who kept me in the here and now and offered unending companionship.

## Waves

We sit like a large boulder just off shore,
    Our problems crash over us in waves,
      until we are submerged,
        seeing only what covers us.
Then in a rhythm determined by nature,
    created by a power greater than us,
      the troubled waters retreat;
        we again breathe fresh clean air.
The water remains peaceful for a while,
    then suddenly rushes over us again.
Like the stable grounded boulder,
    we can trust the natural rhythms and forces,
      remaining steadfast, knowing the waves
        will not grow too great.

# *Introduction*

This book evolved from my own quest for personal healing. My journey has progressed towards healing all my life, though random and undirected at the start. Then I made a conscious choice to begin healing myself in a more focused manner. The art depicted in this book portrays my journey to rediscover myself and to celebrate not only the person I found, but the pain and joy along the way that makes me who I am.

While doing this artwork, I shared it with other women and was treated to a very special discovery. The women who saw it recognized themselves in my work. They said they felt understood in a deep, meaningful way. Some of the women said they felt their own healing begin and that they no longer felt alone. What began as a scary process to appreciate myself became an avenue to self knowledge and appreciation for other women.

My self growth and learning did not happen in a straight line. As it does for everyone, it was a path with detours, curves, hills, and valleys. There were times when I stepped forward, and others when I fell backward. Each discovery was filled with unknowns and untold rewards. I began by naming my experiences; naming them provided me with an opportunity to:

- Become aware of my reality and bring it into the light.
- Look at my reality in its environment with a more objective perspective.
- Have a choice as to how I allowed these experiences to continue to affect me.
- Transform previous experiences and the energy they held, either positive or negative, into productive forces in my life.

As you move through this book I encourage you to have a support system for yourself. Your support system can be one or more trusted friends, a counselor or therapist, or a support group. You may have experiences or memories you will need to share. I encourage you to show this book to your counselor or therapist (if you have one), so she or he is aware of your choice to use this avenue of healing.

Because this book stems from my personal experience as a white woman in upper Midwestern America, it reflects cultural bias' that cannot be avoided. However, the experiences portrayed remain universal in nature.

# How to Use this Book

There are no rules on how to use this book. You make them up as you go along, using it the way that works best for you. For some that may mean starting at the beginning and working straight to the back. For others it may mean jumping around in the book addressing whatever subject makes sense at the time. Each of us has our own way of searching, learning, and growing. It is best to honor your individual style.

When you sit down to play (I use the word play rather than work, because work carries with it the idea of things being hard and grueling. This does not need to be grueling.) find a quiet comfortable space where you won't be interrupted. Fix your favorite beverage and put on your favorite music. This is your special time and you deserve some comforts around you. Be gentle and loving with yourself as you answer the questions and color the pictures. Your experience is unique and so are your answers.

There are no right or wrong colors for any of the pictures. You may choose to color one picture all one color or go out of the lines and that is all right. In some cases going out of the lines might be just what you need to do. You are in control; do what is right for you. This is an exercise in healing, not creating a masterpiece. Color the faces with your skin tone to reflect who you are. Use crayons, markers, glitter, or paint. Paint with brushes or with your fingers. Play and have fun.

For some of the experiences portrayed, there is a black and white photo of my original art work. The others may have a blank space for you to journal or draw your own pictures. There are questions designed to assist you in self discovery and help you celebrate who you are now, and who you are becoming. If you do not see yourself in some of these pictures, just skip over them. Don't try to fit yourself into one just because it is there.

For each of the dark or heavier experiences in our lives there is always hope to be found. As painful as a situation may have been, or is, there is some life learning that can be claimed from it to enrich your life. This may seem like a strange idea, but once you accept the idea you will gain great rewards. After you color each picture spend some time looking at it and write how you feel about what you see. The last question for each picture focuses on turning our negative perceptions into positive ones. A personal example of a positive learning from a negative experience in my life is: My mother died when I was eleven. Because of that I learned to be self reliant and compassionate concerning death and grief. The goal is to acknowledge the loss and then focus on the benefits. It may take some doing to see the benefits and can be difficult if you are still in the midst of a painful experience. I am not always good at it. With practice it becomes easier.

If at any time what you are doing feels overwhelming, take care of yourself and take a break and talk with someone about how you are feeling. There is no need to push. Being gentle and patient with yourself will actually get you where you want to go quicker. It took years to get where you are, don't expect to heal or understand everything overnight.

**Welcome to your playful journey in healing and hope.**

*"You need to claim the events of your life to make yourself yours."*
Anne Wilson-Schaef

8

# Self Portrait

A few months after I left my ex-husband, I became aware that my artwork was again important to me and I realized that I no longer needed to explain to anyone why it was valid. At first, I painted things that were safe, such as landscapes and barns. Then, I completed this self portrait for which I was very proud. I did not dare let anyone know how proud I was because my self esteem was delicate and I was afraid it would be destroyed by someone's criticism of my technical abilities.

Choosing to do a self portrait was a turning point, though I did not recognize it at the time. Over the years, I had grown to believe that I was ugly and choose to stop looking at myself in the mirror or in photographs because of the shame I felt about how I looked. I looked in the mirror only at the parts I needed to—like my teeth when I was brushing them or my hair to comb it. I did not want to look at all of me.

To draw this picture I had to not only look in the mirror, I had to study a photograph of myself for some time and concentrate on every detail of my face. In doing so I rediscovered my beauty. To my delight I discovered I had my mothers eyes and her friendly smiling lips. As a child, and many years after her death, I had been told that I looked like my mother. She was a very beautiful woman. At that time, the information was a mixed message. I felt pride in looking like my mother, but I needed my own identity. Now I was finding both - an identity and pride.

This self portrait was the last thing that I signed with any last name for several years. I chose after this portrait to sign my artwork just "Nancy." Nancy was the only identity I could count on. I was no longer able to identify myself with my maiden name, or with my married name, or years later, with my new married name when it came to my artwork. For me, last names felt like a mark of possession or a role I had to play that I did not want. Now, I am able to have a last name and know it does not define me.

*"Women are like tea bags; put them in hot water and they get stronger."*
Helen Keller

Nancy's Clown Character **"Precious"** (1993)

## Humor

A sense of humor, being able to see the lighter side of a situation, is invaluable. Being human we are all bound to make mistakes and blunders. It is unavoidable. Fortunately we are born with the ability to laugh at our errors. A sense of humor allows us to decide how we will react to what is happening. That's not to say everything is funny while it is happening; many things are not. But within each event lies an opportunity for learning and laugher, even though it may take some time to see it.

I believe each of us have a playful clown living within us. That clown has the ability to see the big picture, to see any situation in its entire environment and to make fun of it. Your clown can keep you from getting too serious and becoming obsessed with the events in your life. Your clown can help you stay playful and light hearted. When you find yourself struggling with something, close your eyes and picture a clown in your situation. Then ask yourself how a clown might respond to the situation.

The humor in our lives is not always positive. Many have experienced negative hurtful humor such as sarcasm, or been the butt of a joke that was too personal. We can choose to let go of those experiences and heal those wounds. Positive humor has a powerful healing effect on us spiritually, physically, emotionally and mentally.

### Precious Humor

To laugh and play freely and make others laugh fills a hole
   in my heart for which I thought there was no hope.
To be a friend to everyone and see the world with new eyes
   is a gift.
It is awesome how Clowning changes frowns to smiles.

Humor through clowning was the greatest doorway to healing.
Laughing at myself broke up my pain and helped me see life
   from a fresh perspective.
I meet others who know how to have fun even when life
   is tough.
I learned laughter helps on every level - spirit, mind and body.

*"A smile is the shortest distance between two people."*
Victor Borge

# Humor

1. Color the hair a wild fun color.

2. Color the face the way you would want your clown character to look.

3. Color the costume with patterns and colors that are fun to you.

4. How old is your clown?

5. What is her name?

6. What is her personality like?

7. What messages about humor did you receive as a child?

8. How would you change any of those messages if you could?

9. Name three people who make you laugh.

10. List 10 things you enjoy doing or that bring you joy (they can be as simple as listening to music). Do at least one every day.

11. Write a statement on how the use of humor could make your life more enjoyable.

## My Refuge

People are scary at times.
    I don't know
       who to trust.
People don't understand
    or are choosing
       not to see.
My four legged friend
    becomes vital
      to my survival.
She listens and snuggles,
    she is gentle
      and never judges.
She looks at me
      with pure admiration
      and offers me
      unconditional
      companionship.

1. Color the cat the same colors as a pet you had, or would have liked to have had.

2. Color the background a color that represents refuge to you.

3. What was the name of a special pet you had? What did it mean to you?

4. Do you have a place of refuge now? Can you create one if you don't have one?

# Despair

Despair and depression are sisters who live together. A visit from them leaves an indelible mark. Once the sisters have visited, a fear may exist that they will return and never leave. It can take a great deal of encouragement and positive experiences to realize they **will** leave and that you are not alone.

When the sisters visit they make themselves at home and you feel drained and tired. They seem to know all your vulnerable places and they magnify your flaws. The sisters are the negative thoughts in your head, constantly reminding you of your failures and your worthlessness. Life with them becomes extremely painful and joy is extinguished. A heavy dark cloud appears to cover everything. Nagging questions come to mind:
> "What is the point?"
> "Why keep trying and going on?"
Then a false idea grows that things will never get better.

The sisters may convince you life is not worth the effort. Despair is the deepest, darkest place anyone can experience. Suicide may seem your only option. **But there are always options** no matter how dark and dismal it may appear at the time. If you are stuck in despair, reach out for help. There are people who want to help you, people who can help you see your options and access them. **There is always hope.** Things can and **will** change for the better.

---

## Despair

The painful howl of a wounded animal
disturbs the still heavy air.

Incomprehensible gloom
drags her into relentless muck.

Sinking, sinking hopelessly
deeper and deeper,
into the gloom of despair.

Powerless to the pervasive gloom,
darkness engulfs her being.

"What is the point?" she cries.
"What is the point?"

---

*"Nothing in life is to be feared. It is only to be understood."*
Marie Curie

13

# Despair

1. Color the background a color that represents despair for you.

2. Color the eyes the same as yours.

3. Color the area of your body black where you feel depression the most.

4. Color the rest of the picture in hopeless colors.

5. When you have experienced depression or despair, what was happening in your life?

6. How do you behave when you are depressed?  Does that action help you feel better or make it worse?

7. List three things you could do to help yourself lift your spirits.

8. What is the most hopeful thing or experience you can think of?  (What we think about causes our feelings.)

9. Name three people you can go to for support.

10. Write a statement about what you have learned about yourself as a result of experiencing depression.

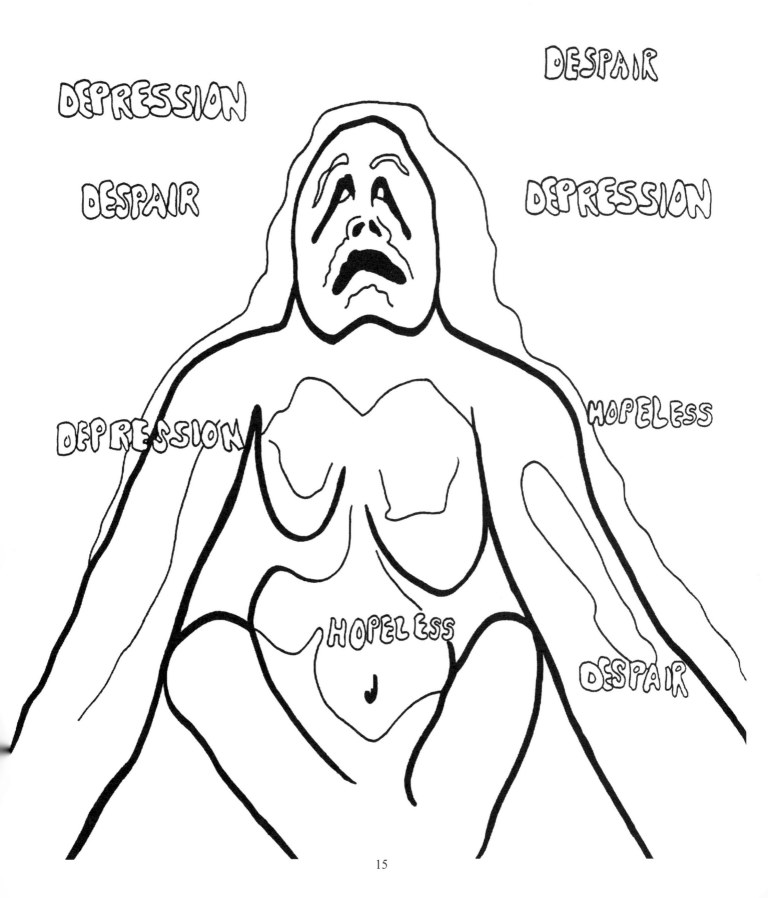

# Keeper Of My Crystal

Lost in an overgrowth of people
      trying to help.
I let them make my decision because
      I believe they know what is best.
I can't take care of myself.
      What do I know about
      anything of importance?
I'm not important, but they are because
      they are not me.
So they keep my crystal - the essence of me.

With time things changed.
      New people have come.
I am asked what my values are.
      "You tell me and I will know."
I am asked what I want from life.
      "You tell me and I will know."

The asking is new.
      They really seem to care.
They await my response.
      But I have none to give.
They continue to wait.
      They won't let me off the hook.

They won't tell me anything
      about what I should do.
They say that I know,
      that I only need to look within.

Slowly I too think maybe
      I might know something.
I share what I think.
      They support what I say!
I have an opinion.
      My strength begins to grow.

*Your thoughts or drawings*

16

# Keeper of My Crystal

Many of us live lost in an overgrowth of people trying to help us. We let other people make decisions for us and we follow what they decide is best for us. After a while we begin to believe we are incapable of taking care of ourselves and that we are not worth much.

We may begin to believe everyone around us knows everything about us. All they have to do is just look at us and they can see how worthless we are. And yet, at the same time, we wonder why they do not see how lonely we are and why they don't help us. The people you have given your crystal to may not even realize they are the "Keeper of your Crystal" or how fragile it may be. You need to be aware of who the keepers of your crystal are and what you want them to do with it.

You may believe you are powerless in changing the situation, that everyone and everything around you is in control and you can do nothing. You may feel that no one believes in you at all.

Trusted friends will help you care for your crystal and help you believe you have purpose and value. However, the key is that those fiends must be willing to accept you for who you are no matter what that may mean at any given moment. They love and accept you even if you're having a bad day or a bad week. You deserve to have your crystal in good hands and well cared for so it can shine brightly.

If, however, you have a belief in a power greater than yourself it can help you move off that position of believing you have no value and don't deserve to be respected. If you can believe your existence in this world has meaning, even if you do not understand what it is or what purpose you are to serve, it can give you the strength to take care of yourself.

*"Each friend represents a world in us,*
*a world possibly not born until they arrive."*
Anais Nin

# Keeper Of My Crystal

1. Color the crystal a color that is bright and shiny to you.

2. Color the area around the crystal a color that you would want around you when you are at your best.

3. Color the trees/people around you that shelter you or that block your light any colors to represent them.

4. How many times have you given your self esteem over to someone else to care for?  Do you realize when you are doing it?

5. Who are the people you give yourself over to?

6. Are you expecting those around you to take care of you?  Are your expectations realistic?  Have you told them what you expect?

7. What are the values they say should be important to you?  Do you agree with them?

8. How many of the trees around you shelter you, and how many are blocking the light?

9. What do you need to do to begin shining your light and let your crystal glow with all of its magnificence?

10. Write a positive statement describing your crystal.

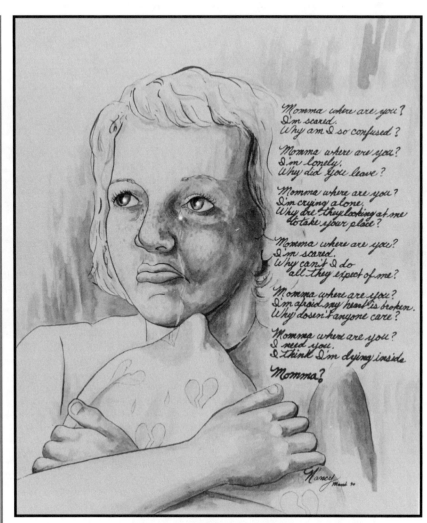

The following text appears within the illustration:

Momma where are you?
I'm scared.
Why am I so confused?

Momma where are you?
I'm lonely.
Why did you leave?

Momma where are you?
I'm crying alone.
Why are they looking at me
to take your place?

Momma where are you?
I'm scared.
Why can't I do
all they expect of me?

Momma where are you?
I'm afraid my heart is broken.
Why doesn't anyone care?

Momma where are you?
I need you.
I think I'm dying inside.

Momma?

## Momma Where Are You?

# Momma Where Are You?

The loss of a parent can take many forms: death, mental illness, physical illness, over commitment, physical or emotional abandonment. A parent does not have to die or go away for child to feel abandoned. Each form of abandonment comes with its own unique pain and personal wounding.

If a child has been abandoned she is likely to experience a lack of support at each stage of life: childhood, adolescence, graduation, birthdays, Mother's Day, holidays, marriage, the birth of a child. Questions about how to handle each new situation life presents, such as an illness, are struggled with. Other unanswered questions echo through her mind like -

"Who am I?"
"Where do I come from?"
"Am I like her?"
"Do I want to be like her?"
"Would she be proud of me?"

She feels sadness for the lost moments of shared tenderness. She feels resentment for having to stand alone against many odds. And she feels grief about not having a mother to share her joy.

One of the greatest impacts of the loss of a mother is the loss of learning social and parenting skills. Mothers often offer the family continuity while role modeling social skills. An abandoned child is at a marked disadvantage which is further emphasized if she is shy or introverted. Unless someone steps in, she may spend the majority of her life standing on the outside wondering how to get in and why she has not been invited.

The abandoned child is not sure how to act and finds it difficult to trust adults. She may become especially sensitive to other's body language and learns to please them. She may learn her role is to serve others and never think of herself.

Roles can be further confused in cases where the child is put in a position of filling the responsibilities of the absent parent. She develops an unrealistic view of what she should be able to accomplish. Her expectations of herself become elevated to a point where it is impossible for her to reach them. She consistently sees herself as a failure and believes deeply that is how everyone else sees her. In her world she can only see what is left for her to do and she rarely acknowledges what she has accomplished.

Out of this difficult struggle she can become creative and self reliant as a result of learning to do the things she is asked to do. Although a part of her feels lost and alone, another part of her has acquired valuable survival skills that have made her strong.

*"For this purpose we have been created: to love and be loved."*
Mother Teresa

# Momma Where Are You?

1.  Color her eyes and hair the same as yours.

2.  Color her shirt a color that most represents innocence for you.

3.  Color the pillow the color that most represents security for you.

4.  Color her tears a color that represents sadness to you.

5.  How do you act when you feel abandoned or unwanted?  Do your actions help you or hinder you?

6.  What have you done to not feel abandoned in the past?

7.  List five new things you could try.

8.  Name a time when you felt abandoned by a parent or significant person.  What form did it come in: death, illness, just too busy, etc.  How old were you?  What did you come to believe about yourself as a result?  Is that belief true?

9.  Write a letter to your inner child reassuring her that any abandonment she may have experienced is not her fault and that you are there for her now.

10. Write a positive statement describing what you have learned about yourself from an experience of abandonment or rejection.

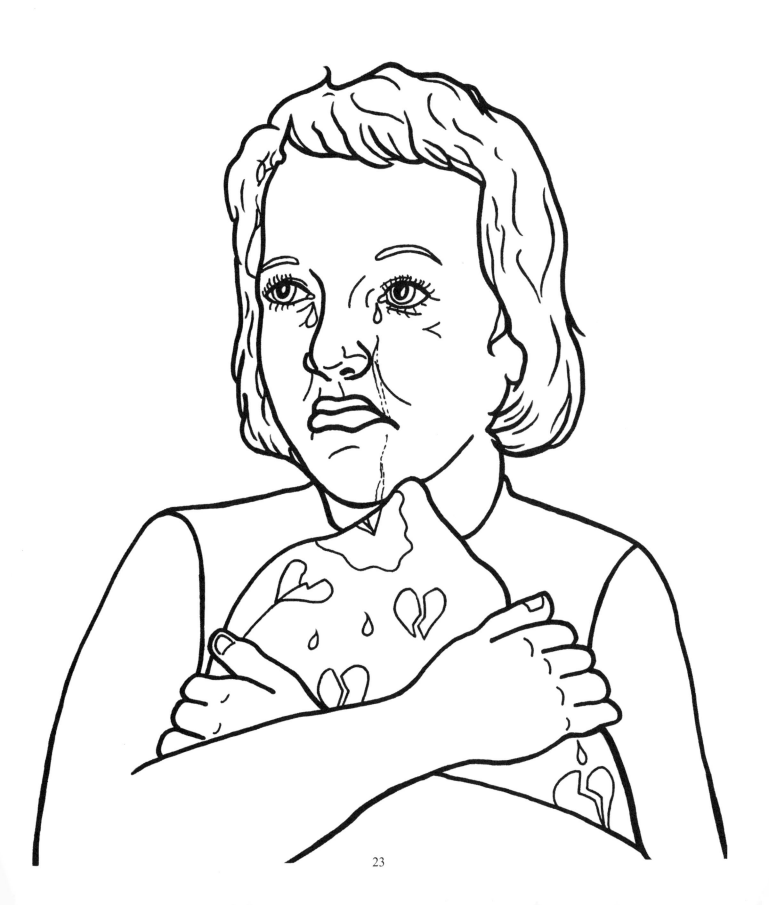

# Inner Child Doll

Much of the healing I had to do dealt with wounds that remained from childhood. Childhood wounds carried forward need special attention to heal and be released. I needed to find a way to communicate with my inner child. I needed to be able to hold her and tell her the things she did not hear as a child that would comfort her and build her self-esteem.

As a child, I did not see or understand the context from which the adults spoke or acted towards me. I could not see that they were trying to protect me, that they were doing the best they could, or that they were carrying their own pain. I needed to be able to reframe and restate the way things were said so their true meaning was clear to me, rather than the misinterpretations of the adult words spoken to an innocent child.

The solution to my challenge was to create this doll in my likeness. I could speak to the doll about things I needed to know when I was younger. I sang to her, danced with her and played with her.

While I was creating her I placed special objects inside her body to symbolize a deep healing. For example, she has a rose quartz in the area of her heart. Rose quartz is said to bring more love into life. She also has a lock of my hair from when I was a child stuffed in her head.

When I was done creating her I took extra time to find the right clothes for her. She has two outfits. The first is a velvet dress similar to one that I wanted as a child but did not get. On the collar is a special angel pin from two of my best friends, my father's union pin and a silver pin from my mother's jewelry box. Her other outfit is a pair of Oshkosh bib overalls. I was quite a tomboy when I was a child and wearing clothes that I could climb trees in and not worry about getting dirty was important to me.

Wrapped carefully around her wrists are a friendship bracelet my daughter made for me, the hospital bracelet from when I was born, and a charm bracelet to which I continue to add treasures. On her feet there are only socks; she hates shoes. She wears Christmas stockings year round because no matter what else was happening in our lives as children, Christmas was always about family and fun.

*"God does not command that we do great things, only little things with great love."*
Mother Teresa

# Inner Child Doll

1. Color the doll's face, eyes and hair like yours.

2. Color her outfit the same colors as a favorite outfit you had as a child.

3. What special objects would you put inside your doll if you made one?

4. What kinds of clothes would you want her to wear?

5. What would you tell her? What did you want to hear as a child but did not, or not enough?

6. Write your doll (inner child) a letter, or draw her a picture depicting what you would have wanted for her to experience if you could change things.

7. Try dialogue journaling with her. Dialogue journaling is much like a dialogue you see in a book. You write a line of conversation, and then she writes a line and you talk back and forth. Try writing with your non-dominant hand for her part of the conversation.

# Braided
## Simplicity

Much healing has been
    accomplished for me
    and my children.
Quietness and simplicity bring
    relief from the past.
I have time now and the ability
    to see the beauty
    surrounding me.
Simple things like
    braided hair,
    playing in the yard with
    unguarded joy,
    watching the children sleep,
    or the sparkle in their eyes.

1. Color her hair to match yours.

2. Color the flowers in her hair joyful colors.

3. Name five things you are grateful for right now.

4. Start a gratitude journal - write down three things you are grateful for every day.

5. Write a statement about how your life will be different when you begin to celebrate the little joys life has to offer.

# Childhood

Childhood is a time for unfettered play and exploration; for swinging, laughing, dancing, spinning, running and singing. It is when dream time and play time merge into one and imagination becomes reality. The environment we are raised in sets the tone for the rest of our lives. Unfortunately, some of us did not get as much play as we really needed. Children learn that either the world is wonderful or scary. If your childhood was not all you wanted, you can rewrite the script. **It is never to late to have a happy childhood.** You can go out and play and explore and rediscover life at any age.

A child is just beginning to learn the rules society has made for her to follow. Her innocence allows her to see the world with a fresh and wonderful perspective. There are possibilities and beauty everywhere for her and everything is an adventure. There is great wisdom in the way a child looks at the world and solves problems. This wisdom still lives within us and you can tap into it.

Most children have imaginary friends. Some grow out of them early. Imaginary friends are great companions. No matter what else is happening, these friends are there for us, to appreciate and accept us, no matter what we do. Some children use their imaginary friends as protectors and guardians which is a creative way to deal with the challenges of life.

Once you get in touch with your child within, your life will feel much fuller and happier. Your child within may need encouragement to come out, especially if she was hurt by the adults in her life. You can teach her that you will be there for her now, and no matter what happens the adult you will protect her. Learning to play again will open the doors to your greatest adventures.

## Childhood

*There was a time when -*

I explored the world freely.
I felt fairies around me
   who whispered secrets in my ear
   and joined me to play
   with my earthy concoctions.
I got dirty and thought I could dig a hole
   all the way through to China.

*But that was before.*

There was a time when
   I knew how to play.
They thought what I did was good
   and that I was cute.
I remember feeling confident
   and open to new things.
I got dirty and climbed trees
   and explored my surroundings.

*But that was before.*

*"Man is most merely himself when he achieves the seriousness of a child at play."*
Herackutus

# Childhood

1. Color her eyes, hair and skin the same as yours.

2. Color her outfit your favorite color as a child.

3. Color her five friends fun and friendly colors.

4. Color the tree house the color you would have wanted it or would have wanted your secret place to be as a child.

5. What was your favorite place as a child? Can you go there or someplace similar now?

6. What was your favorite food as a child? Eat it again soon—and maybe just use your fingers.

7. List three things you enjoyed doing most as a child. Set a goal to do each of them again soon.

8. List five good things that happened to you as a child.

9. Name at least one special adult in your life when you were a child. Can you reconnect with her/him now?

10. Write a positive statement describing what you learned about yourself while growing up.

# Isolation

Isolation can be self imposed or can be imposed by others based on learned behavior and a fear of abandonment. There are as many reasons for feeling isolated as there are lonely people. Isolation can stem from the influence of a single person or from group imposed rules for women to live by. These rules for isolation include:

   Who she can and cannot see.
   Where she can and cannot go.
   What she can and cannot do.
   What she can and cannot eat.
   What she can and cannot wear.

Breaking the rules involves a punishment which may include:

   Leaving her alone.
   Silence.
   Physical abuse.
   Emotional abuse.
   Shaming.

Through isolation a woman learns to obey rules to avoid the punishment or to lessen the isolation. She comes to believe everyone is like the person suppressing her. A fear of complete abandonment grows until she is afraid to speak. Soon she may become afraid to reach out because she expects no one will listen, understand or think she is worth the effort. Fear of further punishment and humiliation immobilizes her. She begins to believe she is invisible and that no one hears her cries.

## Isolation

Eternal blackness engulfs her.
Her face strains with intense agony.

Her mouth held open to scream.
No sound is heard.
Agony is intensified by the silence.

*"Am I invisible?*
*Do they not see me?"*

Tears shed alone eroding a heart.
A heart that only seeks to love.
A heart that only seeks to be loved.

*"Please hear me!*
*Please see me!"*

*"I must be real. The pain is."*

*"God is closer to you than the beating of your own heart."*
Author Unknown

# *Isolation*

1. Color the background a color that feels most lonely to you.

2. Color her tears the color that represents deep pain to you.

3. Color her face a color that represents tension for you.

4. When do you feel the most isolated?

5. Where do you feel the most isolated?

6. When you feel isolated, what is it you would like to see happen? How can you create that?

7. Who are the people you expect to understand and do something about your isolation? Have you clearly told them about your expectations?

8. How do you act when you feel isolated? Does your behavior help or hurt your situation?

9. List five things you could try that are new for you to break the isolation.

10. Write a positive statement about the learning you have had from experiencing isolation.

*Your thoughts or drawings*

**Embraced**

# Embraced

A human embrace is the most life giving experience we share. An embrace has a warm penetrating effect that can begin to soften and heal old wounds. Being embraced offers a deep sense of security, tenderness, and acceptance. We have not all been lucky enough as children to have adults in our lives who are able to give us the positive physical attention we need to grow healthy and strong. Some children have experienced touch as negative and uncomfortable.

Letting another person that close requires a degree of trust if it is not something that has been a part of your life. Begin by allowing yourself to be hugged more by the people you feel safe with and build your sense of trust. Soon you will realize a strong embrace offers protection; it can make the monsters that have lurked under the bed and in the closet disappear.

Hugging is a simple gift given to another that acknowledges and nurtures them. Giving hugs will get you hugs in return. From an embrace, the world is a wondrous and loving place.

## Embraced

Filled up and loved.
A human embrace is the most life
    giving experience we can share.
But because not all touch has been
    good, the experience can be
    negative and uncomfortable.
When trust was built,
    a warm embrace penetrated
    my heart to soften and heal
    the wounds.
Embraced, I feel safe, accepted,
    comforted and loved
    and the world becomes a
    beautiful place.

*"Some people come into our lives and quickly go.*
*Some stay for awhile and leave footprints on our hearts.*
*And we are never, ever the same."*
Flavia

# Embraced

1. Color the woman's clothes a color that makes you feel most secure.

2. Color the background with colors that make you feel hopeful, loved, and excited about the world.

3. List some of the significant people in your life that you could go to for a hug, or to get acknowledgment as a child.

4. What were the rules about touching and hugging when you were a child? Do you still function from those same rules? Do they fit for who you are now?

5. How do you act and feel now when someone approaches you to hug you?

6. List two ways to say "No" to a hug or affection that is not wanted. Practice them so you can use them when you need to.

7. Name two people that you could hug on a daily basis.

8. What is the warmest, safest place you can think of? Describe it in detail. Then practice going there in your imagination. While you are there, get all the affection and hugs you need.

9. Name two ways to ask for affection when you need it. Practice them so you can use them easily when needed.

10. Write a positive statement about what you have learned from the affection or lack of affection you have received in your life.

## The Race Of Denial

Eternally racing, moving,
     terrified death will catch her.
Never slowing,
     never slowing her pace.

Towing, dragging life's burdens,
     vague life learning.
Not seeing or feeling.

She believes she leaves it all behind,
     the pain,
          the fear,
               the failures,
                    the rejection.

Her focus is flawed,
     grossly limited.
She earnestly searches,
     reaching for her illusion.

Striving for tomorrow,
     now and past are meaningless.
Dreams are made of tomorrows,
     because life begins tomorrow.

Glimpses of present joy,
     accomplishments and learning.
Precious gifts of who she is -
     Denied.
          Rejected.
               Discarded.

# Race of Denial

Some women become afraid to see what is around them and learn to deny their experiences, both good and bad. They walk a path that is survival oriented. Getting on this path does not happen all at once; it builds over time. It started with focusing on something that needed her attention, then another, and then another and another. Time passed and more demands were added. Now she stays so busy she does not see how many things she really carries or that what she has yet to do may be unrealistic.

She focuses only on her future, which is held out of reach in front of her. She focuses on tomorrow. She believes tomorrow life will be better. Stopping and really looking at her life is terrifying so she runs endlessly toward her future where she believes life will offer her the things she wants.

Two major losses come from this self-denial. First, accomplishments become unimportant. She cannot see what she has done so far and as a result does not give herself credit for what she has accomplished. There-fore she sees herself as incompetent when in fact she is far from it. The only thing that matters to her is the list of things yet to be done.

Second, her joy is lost. Joy is tossed aside and forgotten along with her accomplishments. They lie discarded and devalued along her path. A woman on the race of denial lives only to survive today with expectations that somewhere in her far off tomorrows life will be better. For her, now is simply to be survived.

*"Often people attempt to live their lives backwards:*
*they try to have more things, or more money, in order to do more of what they want so they will be happier.*
*The way it actually works is the reverse.*
*You must first be who you really are, then do what you need to do, in order to have what you want."*
Margaret Young

# Race of Denial

1. What color is your - Past, Present, Future? Color those words to reflect those colors.

2. What color best represents burden for you? Color the backpack that color.

3. Choose a color for each word that you feel best fits with its meaning.

4. List past and current:
   - Things you consider broken dreams.
   - Times you felt rejected or abandoned.
   - Situations you see as your failures.
   - Disappointments in your life.

5. List past and current fulfilled dreams (these things need not be big items):
   - Times you were accepted or welcomed and by whom.
   - Your successes or when you had a sense of accomplishment.
   - Times you felt joy.

6. If all you had was now/today, how would you do things differently. What would be really important to you?

7. List what you have done in the past to reclaim and give yourself credit for what you have accomplished.

8. List the items you want to reclaim and stop denying. (The good things in your life.)

9. List five things you could do to begin to reclaim all of who you are.

10. Name the strengths you have gained from your past experiences. Write a statement that says how you are stronger because of them.

Your thoughts

## Immobilized

Poised to run, anxious for life to begin,
     her heart pounds,
       she awaits her gates opening.
She knows who she is,
     adrenaline surges through her veins.
She sees possibilities.

Her companion stands near,
     She too awaits her gates opening.
Muscles ache with anticipation,
     to freely express her power and grace.
Suddenly her companion breaks free,
     seeing the gate for the illusion it is.

She remains frozen,
     her gate remains
     her illusion holds firm.
Fatigue from waiting,
     continuous effort.
She is discouraged.

Slowly she retreats into the gloom,
     all diligent effort thwarted,
     identity fading.
Her purpose is again clouded.

A familiar pattern - retreat.

The gate an illusion,
     founded in flawed beliefs,
Self imposed limitations.

She is blinded to possibilities,
     to options.

She could join her companion
     dancing in the invigorating
     fields of the world.

But no.
She succumbs.
     Destructive patterns continue.

# Immobilized

It is human nature to resist change. In the past, women have received little or no encouragement to move forward. When you or someone else puts up additional barriers you can become immobilized.

There is comfort in having things remain the same. You know what to expect. Change can mean work and it can feel too difficult. Your body and mind remember how hard it was the last time  you made a change and you want to stop, because you feel tired just thinking about it. Succumbing to that tired feeling and fear of change continues patterns of behavior that may be destructive. You tend to repeat behaviors because they are familiar and comfortable. Like your favorite pair of jeans; they have served you well, but it may be time to give them up.

These restrictions and barriers are learned. What is learned can be unlearned. Part of what you learn is to be sensitive to subtle cues from others as to what is right or wrong. You make assumptions about the subtle clues and equate some of them to how much you are valued. Then your self-esteem is negatively affected.

When you begin to see yourself as worthwhile, you become less sensitive to outside cues and influence. When self-esteem is high you begin to take risks and learn you can survive and succeed and become less immobilized. The restrictions and barriers become less and less threatening. Most of them turn out to have less power over you than you imagined.

Taking risks teaches you more about who you are and you grow stronger. You can then move into new areas of life, perhaps ones you have long wanted to experience. These changes offer an excitement of future possibilities for fun and fulfillment. Change makes you feel vital and alive.

*"Do what you feel in your heart to be right—for you'll be criticized anyway. You'll be damned if you do, and damned if you don't."*
Eleanor Roosevelt

# Immobilized

1. What color is your gate?  Who put it there or how was it created?

2. Think of a time when you were excited to do something but didn't do it:
   - What or who stopped you?
   - What thoughts were rolling through your mind?
   - Where do you think you learned those ideas?
   - Would you teach your child the same things?

3. Can you think of a time you retreated?  How did that feel?  What did you tell yourself?

4. What field do you want to be running in?  Where do you want to be?  What is stopping you?

5. How do you act when you are immobilized?

6. Who in your life has done what you wish you could do?  Talk with them and find out how they did it and use them as a role model.

7. List what you have tried in the past to get yourself moving.

8. List five things you could try next time to get yourself moving on something you want to do.

9. If you could do anything, no limits, what would it be?

10. Write a statement about what you have learned from your past immobilization.

# Woman Warrior

Many women carry a false belief that they are weak and powerless. They have become convinced they have no control over what happens to them. Living in fear and having low self-esteem makes this seem to be true.

We are all born strong and powerful. Living deep within each woman is a strength she can call upon at any time. It may seem weak or like a distant dream at first, but it can easily grow strong.

Connecting with our strong side may seem scary and threatening. Meeting your inner warrior is a process of unfolding – it happens at different speeds for each woman. Bringing her out does not mean you are going to have to fight. A true warrior knows gentleness is truly the stronger way. It is more about acknowledging your strength and power in any situation. Your warrior is there to remind you during difficult times that you are capable and wise.

In the drawing the warrior has a variety of religious symbols pictured on her: Christianity, Judaism, Goddess, Native American, the Infinity symbol and a crystal ball. This is not meant to represent all of the religions of the world. The symbolism portrays our coexistence as humans. We all seek our purpose and meaning from our source. There are similarities in various beliefs and wisdom to be shared that can bring peace to all. There are an unlimited number of things we can learn from each other, if we remain open. We walk different paths together toward the same goal.

The warrior is the strong woman who lives within, whom you can rely on and trust. She is connected to the creative source and therefore does not walk in fear. A key to finding and knowing her is trusting that she is real – no matter what you have been told. Then start trusting your intuition and believing in yourself. Before you know it, you will be standing stronger.

---

## Woman Warrior

Deep within her core, woman has intuitive Knowing, a nurturing, life-giving power embracing her spirit.

*Behold......her Warrior.*

She knows no religious barriers because each is a part of her.
She knows little of deliberate destruction.
To protect and survive, her energy awakens to fight.

*Vigilantly she guards.*

Grounded in the spiritual forces of Mother Earth's strength, change and transformation.

*Embrace her.     Trust her.     Call upon her.*

---

*"You are not here as a human being having a spiritual experience.*
*You are a spiritual being having a human experience."*
Wayne Dyer

# Woman Warrior

1. Color her clothes a color that makes you feel strong.

2. How do you feel about your warrior? Do you have fear or apprehension about her coming out?

3. Are you aware she is your strong and confident side?

4. What issues or circumstances would motivate you to fight?

5. What is the religion of your family of origin? Are you currently practicing it or any other form of spirituality?

6. Do you have biases about other religious beliefs? If yes, what are they? How might they get in the way of communication and sharing with others?

7. In what types of situations do you feel strong? What have you done in the past to bring out your strength?

8. List five ways you could practice coming from your strength and confidence.

9. Describe yourself as if you were acting from a place of complete confidence. Practice acting that way in your life.

10. Write a positive statement about yourself concerning your courage and strength.

# Shame

Tormented from the strain,
     she struggles to hold back the pain.
Imposed shame presses down.
     Dutifully she carries the weight of
     the world.
Unable to lift her head,
     to see beauty, to see possibilities.
Under shame,
     the world is ugly, hurtful, dusty,
     dirty and disgusting.

Of course she is ashamed,
     *she is woman*
          *it must be her fault.*

To let it go could be easy,
     it could just roll off.
*Couldn't it?*

Who's powerful fist holds her down?
  **S**  trangers
     briefly touching her life.
  **H**  umanity
     despising it's flaws.
  **A**  ncestors and traditions
     long since gone.
  **M**  embers of her earthly family
     and treasured friends.
  **E**  ven her own
     unrealistic expectations.

She acquired great strength
     carrying the load.
Strong muscles that could be used
     for positive things.

**If Only.**

**Shame**

46

# Shame

Rare is the woman who escaped the influences of shame as a child. For some there is a sense that just being a woman is something to be ashamed of. Shame is a sickness that plagues both women and men, but has been used to control women in epidemic proportions for centuries.

Shame has traditionally been an accepted way of disciplining our children. It is based on a lie that you somehow have less value because of something you did or something about you. We use it because our parents used it on us and their parents used it on them. Most people who use shame to discipline and control have no idea of how damaging it is. The shame they inflict is often well intended and is meant to help you. Some do not realize they are even shaming another person with what they are saying or what they are doing.

No matter what the intent, the price of shame is too dear. There is no redeeming value to shame. It cuts to the core and destroys self-esteem, faith, hope, and sense of purpose leaving little or no creative energy.

In shame, the world is ugly and hurtful. It is difficult to see any beauty or believe good and beauty are deserved in your life. Soon the shaming becomes integrated and we shame ourselves when we don't meet our own expectations, realistic or not.

Carrying shame and moving on with life requires great strength. This strength can be re-channeled in more positive directions and become an asset. To address shame, we begin by looking within and accepting all that we find. You begin by practicing and then acquiring a deep knowledge that you are perfect just as you are and that shame serves no purpose in your life. Those who impose it on you were wrong. You have a choice about letting shame go or keeping it.

*"One of the most striking differences between a cat and a lie is that a cat only has nine lives."*
Mark Twain

# Shame

1. Where do you feel shame in you body?  Color that area black on her body.

2. Color the sky a shade that most makes you think of shame.

3. Color the ground she stands on the color of muck.

4. What in your past are you most ashamed of?  Ask yourself this: if a dear friend came to you with that same thing, how would you treat her?  Would you forgive her?  Now do the same for yourself.

5. Who or what holds you down? (strangers, society, church, ancestors, traditions, family, friends) How do they hold you down?

6. What expectations for yourself hold you down?  What are you willing to do to let go of those expectations?

7. What effect does being ashamed have on you spiritually, physically, emotionally, or in your relationships?

8. Do you have a belief that somehow because you are a woman you are second rate?  Is that really true?

9. How do you act when you are ashamed?  What have you done to stop feeling shameful?

10. Write a statement of how acknowledging the shame in your life has helped you learn more about who you are and how that can make you stronger.

## Caribbean Fantasy

I dream of escaping
    anywhere but here.
I dream of escaping
    to a romantic tropical place.
I dream of palm trees
    and ocean breezes.
I dream of escaping where
    no one knows me.

I dream of swimming in an aqua
    sea with exotic fish.
I dream of basking in
    the nurturing sun.
I dream of a magnificent gentle
    man serving me while
    I lounge in a hammock.
I dream that when his eyes meet
    mine his smile tells me
    I am gorgeous.

I dream of escaping

1.  Color the mask vibrant tropical colors.

2.  If you could escape:
        Where would you go?
        What would you do there?
        Would you be alone?

3.  What would you be searching for in your escape?

50

# Candle In The Dark

Hope begins small, like the flickering flame of a candle. It may come from within or begin with the helping hand of another. It only takes one person to make a world of difference. It can be as simple as a smile acknowledging your presence or an attentive ear honestly listening to what you have to say.

Hope is an ember that can be nurtured and have life breathed into it. It can become a fire that clearly lights and warms your way.

One candle standing alone does not illuminate many possibilities. Support from others is key to turning your ember into a flame. Candles coming together can light up the universe.

Once your candle is lit, turn and light another's by offering a helping hand. Even a small effort can have an enormous impact, like ripples on the water from a pebble tossed into a calm pool. You may never see how far a simple effort can go or how deeply it will affect another person's life. Each time you offer another person help you feel stronger, capable and more hopeful. The outcome of your assistance is not what is important. <u>It is your intention</u> to assist another <u>that makes the difference </u>for you.

## Candle In The Dark

Displayed with lovely acceptance
    an inner glow shines outward.

Her candle is one of many -
    unique colors,
    unique sizes,
    unique shapes,
    unique purposes.

Special gifts bloom from within,
    behold beauty unfolding.

Hopes, dreams and pain
    move out of the darkness.

Life is illuminated,
    gently embraced.

*"Every flower must grow through dirt."*
Anonymous

# Candle in the Dark

1. Color the candle the color of hope.

2. Color the area around the flame the color that most represents your dreams.

3. Color the shirt the color that make you feel warm and loved.

4. What dreams do you want to bring into the light?

5. Whose candles around you can add more light to yours and in turn, yours to theirs?

6. What gifts or talents do you have that perhaps you have kept in the dark? What do you need to do to bring them into the light?

7. List the ways you have worked to make your dreams and hopes real.

8. List five more ways you can make your dreams come true.

9. Name three people who can support you in making your dreams real and help you out of the darkness.

10. Write a statement about the strength you have acquired from having lived in the darkness.

# Expectations

Her body painfully distorted
        from the constant pull.
Expectations of others;
        dead, alive, old and new;
        family, friends and strangers.
Draining her life force,
        pulling and sucking endlessly.

*"More, more, they always want more."*

Eyes held closed,
        afraid to see,
        what will be
        the new responsibility.
She peeks to see
        one small piece at a time,
        are they smiling at me?

*"I don't understand.  Why does it hurt?"*

She is blind to the breadth
        of her situation.
She is clear about
        her engulfing feelings,
        the unceasing burden
        of silent excruciating pain.
People are
        eyes, mouths, hands,
        asking, taking, draining.

*Relief is a candle
        whose flame has gone out.*

# Expectations

The expectations put on women by family, friends, children, parents, grandparents, church, school, and society as a whole seem infinite. Many of these expectations are unspoken, others are clearly stated. The expectations are presented as if there is no other choice. Women are systematically taught they have no choice most of the time; the rest of the time, options are extremely limited. This can become learned helplessness with a feeling that "It doesn't matter what I do or try, everyone else comes first." As we learn that other's needs are more important than ours and the others always "should" be tended to first, we also learn to only give what is left over to ourselves.

Because of the expectations of others, we are taught to be all and to do all. Be gorgeous, keep smiling no matter what, be available every hour and minute of the day. No matter what you give, they always seem to want more.

To find relief, some women search for a white knight to rescue them. Once they find him they soon discover that he too has needs and expectations for her. Like denial, we begin to lose sight of how much we are doing, how much people are expecting of us, and what is realistic.

The key to relief from the expectations is to find a balance between what we can do for others and caring for ourselves. Learning is say "No" is a healthy thing for everyone involved. Saying no helps those making the request of us learn limits and begin to respect us. Saying no, we learn to respect and take care of ourselves, which is vital if we want to fully be there for those we love.

*"The minute you settle for less than you deserve, you get even less than you settled for."*
Maureen Dowd

# Expectations

1. Color the body a color that represents feeling exhausted and strained.

2. Color the background a gloomy color or colors.

3. List the expectations others have for you. It may be easier to list them by the various roles you play: mother, sister, daughter, employee, etc. Color the hands and faces colors that represent those expectations.

4. List the expectations you have for yourself—be specific.

5. Review your lists and ask yourself if the expectations are realistic. Would you expect a friend to handle them all?

6. How often do you stop and take an accounting of how much you are doing and let go of some of the demands put on you?

7. What would be the benefits of letting go of some of the responsibilities you have?

8. Are there particular people or places that seem to demand more than others? What can you do about those that are out of balance?

9. Why do you take on so many things? What do you get out of it?

10. List three ways to say "No" to future requests made of you. Practice them so you can use them when you need to.

57

# Creation

You need not give birth to feel the exhilaration of creation. Any creation can be watched, nurtured and felt at a deep meaningful level as it develops. Each creation is truly an awesome experience and an honor to be a part of. Creation comes with responsibility because it affects other people, which may have both positive and negative impacts. Creation may mean the loss of some freedoms, but the rewards outweigh any losses. Each creation is an unfolding of opportunities and hope. Each lets us touch the immortality humans strive for.

It is a special honor to create and bring new life into the world. To hold a newborn baby is to experience the presence of an angel. You look into a bright face full of wonder, trust, honesty and innocence. To raise a child, to wake at night to change, feed, comfort and nurture is to know the reality and awesome responsibility of motherhood. It is a demanding mixed blessing indeed. Like all creations it has both frustrating moments and moments of pure joy.

Our children give us an opportunity to break old unhealthy patterns that may exist in our families. It is an opportunity to start fresh and create hope for a new generation. Just because some family tradition, form of communication or discipline has been handed down through generations, does not mean we are tied to it. If what you learned in your family is not helpful eliminate it and reinforce those things which were handed down that are positive and life giving.

## Creation

New life grows within and
     possibilities unfold before me.
I stand at a turning point.
     Do I embrace the fight
     to break a chain of violence?
     or,
     Do I keep quiet and
     hope for the best,
     squelching possibilities of
     new and better things?

With fervor I choose to embrace
     the challenge for my children's sake.
It's not their fault,
     they should not pay the price
     of choices made by family
     who came before them.

My children give me purpose,
     and become the driving force
     that moves me through my fears.
They tell me I should be doing it
     for myself, but
     I value them more than me.

*"Your children are not your children.*
*They are the sons and daughters of Life's longing for itself."*
Kahlil Gibran

# Creation

1. Color her dress the color of creativity and new life.

2. Color the walls the color you would want a room to be to welcome a new creation.

3. In the window, draw or color something that is inspiring to you.

4. What, if any, negative messages do you want to eliminate that are traditionally passed down in your family?

5. What positive messages do you want to either replace the old with, or add?

6. If you could only change one thing for your children, what would it be? How will you do that?

7. What dream or goal do you have for yourself? Where do you keep this treasure and what do you need to do to give birth to it?

8. What do you see as the biggest road block to attaining your dream? What can you do about it?

9. What sacrifices would you make for your creation to be nurtured and grow? How do you cherish and nurture your creations?

10. If you could create anything and had no limits set on you, what would it be?

# Body Reclamation

Start with a religious up bringing where
    the body is professed to be dirty
    and shameful.
Add verbal and physical battering
    with a smattering of disgust
    and threats of harm.
Add media's revered beauties
    who are thin,
    sleek and endowed.
Mix it all together
    and the message is clear -

THIS BODY IS TRASH!

**Body Reclamation** was an exercise in reclaiming the imperfect beauty of a body that had experienced many physical and emotional violations. It is a plaster body cast of my torso that was then decorated. It is a celebration of hurtful words loosing their power, while joyful color and texture replace the scars.

1.    Color the body a color that represents warmth and acceptance to you.

2.    Color the shawl a color that represents forgiveness to you.

3.    What hurtful words did you hear about your body? Know that they are not true.

4.    Write a letter to "them" about how they were wrong in not seeing the beauty that is inherent in who you are.

# The Pedestal

Women are expected to be perfect in our society. We are expected to be beautiful in thought, action and body. We are compared to a fictitious woman on a pedestal who is pure, flawless and unrealistic.

This expectation leaves us striving to get on and stay on the pedestal of perfection. It starts at an early age with toys like Barbie dolls. Barbie is better than perfect: her figure, her coloring, her complexion, clothes and hair all exemplify beauty. The learning about what is expected continues in what we see in TV commercials, magazine and newspaper ads, in movies and more. Just about everywhere we turn we are reminded how we are to be. The perfect woman has:

> A tiny waist.
> Full and round breasts
>   (no sag allowed).
> Tight buttocks, round and not too large.
> Long, slender and shapely legs.
> Delicate soft hands with perfectly shaped
>   and painted nails.
> Large round eyes with long lashes.
> Moist full lips.
> Soft shiny hair that smells terrific.
> Flat stomach.
> Straight white teeth.
> Fresh and alluring scent.
> Friendly soothing voice.
> Sweet and accommodating disposition.

No woman on Earth has or ever will meet all those criteria. Not even some of the time. The difficult part is that the messages are subtle and we begin to believe there is something wrong with us because we don't measure up. The truth is "There is nothing wrong with the way we look."

Generally, it is the men in our lives who encourage or demand us to be the woman on the pedestal. But other women can be just as responsible. We try to please men in particular, disregarding who we are and what we need. Men are no different when it comes to what they have learned we should be. They have been taught to expect women to be a certain way as well. They are reacting from the same societal rules women have been exposed to.

The woman on the pedestal is not real. Our attempts to be her will always fail. The price we pay in an effort to become her is too high. We need to see the beauty in the body we were given – the beauty is there. We need to see who we are inside and appreciate what we find. We need to spend time with people who accept us for who we are. There is no need to change for anyone else, we have been created perfect just the way we are.

*"I don't confuse greatness with perfection. To be great anyhow is…*
*the higher achievement."*
Lois McMaster Bujold

# The Pedestal

1. Color the pedestal a color that makes you feel hopeless.

2. Color the woman on the top of the pedestal the colors of perfection and light.

3. Color the girl climbing the pedestal the colors of great effort.

4. How do you feel about your hair, smile, complexion, height, figure, sex or breast size? Ask yourself whose rating scale you are using.

5. Name at least two physical features about you that you like.

6. Describe perfection. Where did that definition come from? Who influenced it? Are you trying to be that definition?

7. What do you think life would be like if you were perfection? Would you really want that life?

8. List the things that you value in another person, the things that attract you to them (not just the physical aspects). The list you create will be the same values you possess.

9. List five qualities about yourself that you are most proud of.

10. Write a positive statement about what you have learned from trying to be perfect, or trying to be what someone else wanted you to be. This is a quality that you can claim as your own.

# The Pedestal

She is beautiful.
    She is wonderful.
        She is honored.
            She is everything.

*She IS Perfection.*

She is what I *should* be.
    But it seems insurmountable.
        I'm nothing until I get there.
        I'm doing my best,
            Why can't I reach the top?
                He says I should be up there.

*What's wrong with me?*

Is that really me up there?
    Am I supposed to be her?
        Is that what he expects?

*Could it be too much?*

It is the pinnacle of futility.
    For if the top is reached;
        her true inner beauty,
            her soul inspired wonder,
                her cherished honor, is lost.
Everything real is lost.

*She is nothing.*

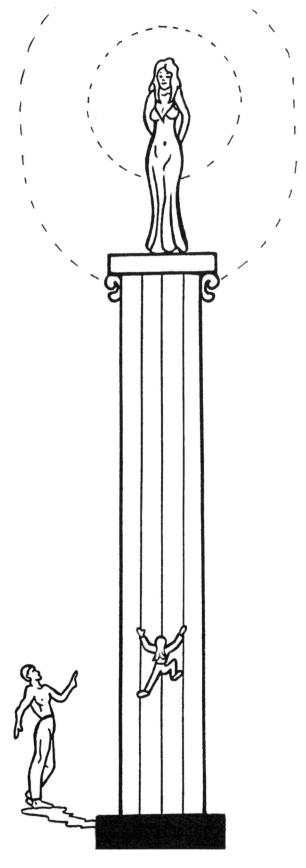

# Rainbow Vision

If I could change my face
    I would make it bright rainbow
    colors with eyes that sparkle
    and glow.

My mouth would be veiled with
    a filter that would allow me
    to speak only the truth and
    never negatively about others.

Angel dust would sprinkle my words
    so they would bring
    only healing and joy.

Everyone that looked at me would
    see compassion and beauty
    reflected back at them.

They would see the good in
    themselves,
    others around them
    and the world.

If I could change my face.

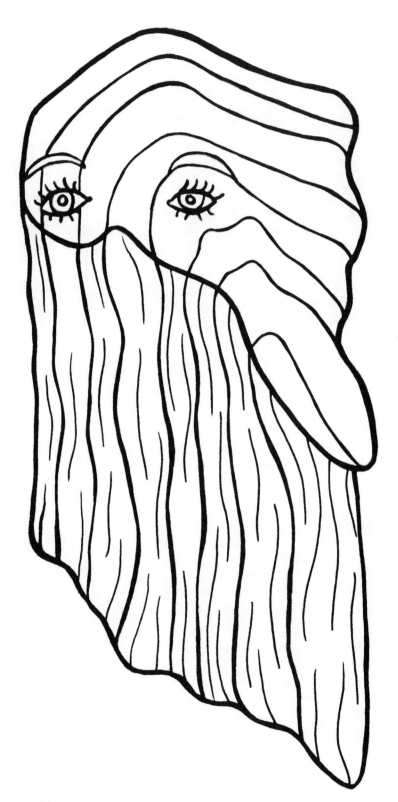

1.  Color the mask colors of the rainbow.

2.  What changes would you make in how
    you talk to people?

3.  What changes would you make in how
    you treat people?

4.  How do you think your life would be
    different if compassion was the main
    part of every interaction you had with
    people.

# Singing Her Truth

Singing your truth stems from paying attention to what you know, when you know it, and realizing you know it. Acknowledging those moments in your past when you did it "right," were able to help another person, or just knew what to do in a given situation can help you discover your greatness. These moments of greatness can empower you and thrust you forward. These moments tell the world who you truly are. Everyone may not agree with you about your moments of greatness and that is all right, your opinion counts. With time you may even begin to enjoy the challenge and growth that stems from discussions of opposing opinions.

Your truth comes from your depths. It is who you are. To reach it may mean you must forgive yourself and others for the big stuff and all the little things. It means valuing difference no matter what. It is understanding that it is the differences between people that gives life richness.

Singing your truth does not mean using it to harm others in any way. To sing your truth is to be gentle. There is no place for sarcasm or demanding statements in truth. It means celebrating who you are, your talents and what you know. It means celebrating who your friends and family are and sharing their celebrations. Singing your truth means asking for what you need and knowing you deserve it. It means reaching for your star because you can and are meant to.

## Singing Her Truth

Joyful courage has arisen.
She bursts forth in truth-filled song
which acknowledges -
    her beauty,
    the distance she as traveled,
    the power she knows she posses,
    the lessons she has learned.

Life is not perfect and never will be.

The song is her personal journey,
    her choices,
    her opportunities lost and taken,
    her tragedies and triumphs.

She will no longer let them have her believe
    she is wrong while they are always right.

She has seen both sides now and knows
    there is truth for both
    and each person from their perspective.

She is singing her truth.
Celebrating her life and all that she has been,
    all that she is and
    all that she will be.

*"Beginning today, I will use the power of my love to create a masterpiece of art—my own life."*
Author Unknown

# Singing Her Truth

1. Color the streams flowing from her mouth colors that are hopeful and promising to you.

2. Color all the different symbols joyous colors.

3. Color her hair, eyes and skin the same as yours.

4. What have you wanted to say but have been unable to?

5. Can you think of a time you wanted to speak up but did not?  What stopped you?  Did it turn out that you were right?

6. What would be different for you if you began to say what you think and know?  Would you get what you need?

7. List three important people in your life.  Name something you appreciate about each of them.  Now make a point to share that information with them.

8. Write a statement about your most powerful skill or talent.

9. Write three positive statements (affirmations) about yourself.  Say these to yourself each day in the mirror for three weeks or more.

10. Write a positive statement about what you learned from not speaking your truth in the past.

**Your thoughts**

# The Way Things
# Should Have Been

I watch the boys play
    and do all kinds of fun stuff.
Girls can't do that I am told,
    we have our "own" fun stuff.
We have our stupid dolls and playing
    dress up so we look good for the boys.
It doesn't seem fair

I'm grown now and the boys still
    get to do all kinds of fun stuff.
Women can't do that we are told we have our
    "own" fun stuff like children and cleaning.
He goes off with the guys
    on adventures big and small.
They drive away laughing
    returning hours later boasting of their conquests.
I bore them when I interject my adventures of
    potty training, teething and laundry galore.

Girls and women should be able to
    go on adventures big and small.

Dumb rules about who's fun stuff is who's
    are going to be broken

1. Chose one of the girls that looks like she is having the most fun and color her to represent you.

2. Color the others playfully.

3. Color the water a safe color.

4. What are some of the things you wanted to do but could not because you are a girl?

5. Write a statement about how life would be if there were no barriers around roles.

**Your thoughts or drawings**

*"If one desires a change, one must be that change before that change can take place."*
Gita Bellin

# Loneliness

For many, being alone is the most difficult experience. For some women, being in a roomful of people is when she feels her loneliest. If people are not paying attention to her or make the first move to connect with her she feels invisible and unimportant. Many women believe they are the only ones who feel alone and that no one could possibly understand the depth of their pain. Some believe that no one wants them even as a friend because of their feelings of loneliness.

Another possible outcome of loneliness may be a growing belief she is a burden, that somehow she will ruin everyone else's fun and they do not want her around because of it. A lonely woman is scared to let people too close. She may say "no" to an invitation when her heart is saying "yes." Life has taught her to be wary of everyone and sadly it becomes easier to remain lonely than risk the rejection she thinks is inevitable.

If she is in a relationship there is nothing more painful than lying in bed with her partner, a person who says he loves her, but won't talk to her. He doesn't want to hear what she has to say. She can't understand what is wrong and she comes to believe it is all her fault.

She can't see that the loneliness in other people is what may be causing them to keep their distance from her. She sees only the masks that other people wear and believes them to be real. Those around her may need to reach out to her over and over before she will let them close.

## Loneliness

A heart bleeds as its life force leaves.
She reaches to touch and receives not much.
Pain engulfs her.

A young woman reaches from the core of her
    being, to touch someone she believes
    sees her.
She is unable to make the connection.

A child's arms held open to parents whose
    busy lives hide the burdens of
    their own loneliness.
No response.

Pain and isolation continue.
A destructive tradition passed through
    generations.

Within a desolate dark shell she lives naked
    and closed off.
Paralyzed with fear she denies the
    crippling pain.

Outside her desolate shell bright faces
    seem to see her.
No one moves to touch her.

To touch her, to see her,
To know her pain, to share her pain,
Means risking their own struggle with denial.

*The experience is painfully multiplied!*

*"Loneliness, a common human experience we share separately."*
Nancy Scheibe

# Loneliness

1. Color the cave she sits in the color that represents isolation to you.

2. Color the area around the outside of the cave colors that represent the joy and fun you see everyone else having when you feel lonely.

3. Color the tears the color of loneliness.

4. Do you think your parents, or other significant adults, were lonely when you were a child?
   How much do you know about what your parents experienced?
   How might their experiences have effected yours?

5. Who, as a child, did you want to notice you and give you attention that did not?
   What message did you get from that experience?
   Do you think that message is really true?

6. Who, as a young woman, did you not get attention from that you wanted?
   What message did you get from that experience?  Is it true?

7. How do you act when you are feeling lonely?  Do those behaviors help you feel better or make it worse?

8. List five positive things you can do to get out of feeling lonely.

9. Name three people that you could call when you feel lonely.

10. Write a positive statement about what you have learned from your experiences of being lonely.

## Laughing Crone

When I am old I will have lived.
    I will have known many pains and delights.
    I will have known many challenges great
       and small.
    I will have known many failures
       and triumphs.
    I will have loved and learned.
    I will have experienced compassion
       and terror.

When I am old I will have acquired a wise
       one's perspective.
    I will have risen above the human
       limitations that cloud our perspective
and understanding.

When I am old I will smile at adversity.
    I will know "this too shall pass" and
       "time heals."
    I will know there is more to our world
       than just my perspective.

When I am old my laughter will flow freely
       and my joy will be contagious.

1. Color her with tenderness and joy.

2. What are your expectations for when you are older?

3. What are your expectations for you acquiring wisdom?

4. Write a statement about what you want for yourself when you are older—put no limits on yourself as you write your statement.

# Enough

Your thoughts

# Enough

Enough is a place of true self-acceptance. It is a place where peace of mind grows and is nurtured.

Unfortunately, Enough can seem an illusive state of mind; an illusive destination. When the path you follow seems to double back or you find yourself repeating old behaviors it is easy to think you have lost it all. All the work, pain, and progress seem like wasted effort. But no growth or self-care effort is ever a waste or loss.

Once you find Enough she will never leave you. She is the one who will automatically know, understand, and forgive all your human failings. She has a sense of humor about herself and sees life from a greater perspective. She knows you are doing the best you can with what you have and what you know.

It is only your own limiting beliefs that cause you to lose sight of Enough; she never loses sight of you because she is your connection to the divine. You never have to struggle alone again because she lives within you. She is who you truly are. She is your soul and your spirit made in perfection.

*"When we do the very best we can, we never know what miracle is wrought in our life, or in the life of another."*
Helen Keller

## Enough

It's been a difficult struggle to find Enough.
    She's climbed mountainous high peaks
    and walked dark and gloomy valleys.
The journey circled her back to her beginning,
    back to her creation.

She learned to listen too well to them
    and drowned in their limitations of her.
The journey's been painful and difficult.
    At times she wished she'd never begun.
But once that first step was taken
    there was no turning back.
The veil of denial lifted,
    her shell cracked open to a ray of hope.

She pushed onward not knowing her destination,
    at times it was unbearably painful, others
    exceptionally joyful.
Uncertainty lurked around each corner,
    each step was terrifying.

Slowly at first,
    she began to see the other side of terror.
Well hidden were greater rewards
    than she ever imagined.
A beauty that existed in the world
    was becoming part of her world.
Time that painfully took forever,
    passed suddenly and was gone.
The pain, disappointments and falling backwards,
    Were well worth it.

She discovered it was she who is Enough,
    a truth no one could take away.
Stretching her arms like a transformed butterfly,
    she unfolds to greet the world.
She knows a beauty so deep and awesome that only
    the power who bestowed it on her knows
    its true depth.

Joy, excitement and power overwhelm her.
Moving from Enough's power she shares it
    with others.

**Enough is our spiritual being
    who never loses sight of us –
    it is we who lose sight of her.**

# Enough

1. Color her skin, hair, and eyes to match yours. Feel free to draw clothes on her to match the style you would like to wear.

2. Color the butterfly bright hopeful colors.

3. Color the sky bright and full of possibilities.

4. Name some of the mountains that you have climbed in your journey.

5. Describe your first steps to get healthy or change your situation. Celebrate each one of them.

6. What kept you moving forward when things got really tough?

7. What were the first rewards you received for taking your journey to yourself?

8. What are some of the new behaviors you have, or want, or are beginning to develop as a result of working from Enough's power?

9. List five things you can do on a regular basis to celebrate yourself. (It may be as simple as soaking in the tub.)

10. Name three people who have helped you along the way and thank each of them.

11. Write a positive statement that describes who you are. Include all the positive characteristics you have discovered. Read it out loud to yourself daily.

**Your thoughts or drawings**

*"I keep the telephone of my mind open to peace, harmony, health, love, and abundance.*
*Then, whenever doubt, anxiety, or fear, try to call me, they will keep getting*
*a busy signal-and soon they'll forget my number."*
Edith Armstrong

# Conclusion

We walk this Earth and experience many challenges, joys, pains, and special moments. It is just part of being human. From the outside some lives appear to be perfect, healthy and happy while others seem damaged and plagued with bad luck. Some people seem able to rise above what life hands them and others crushed by it. No matter what your experience has been up to now, or will be in the future, you have a choice as to how you respond to it. You decide how it will affect you emotionally and otherwise. No one can predict what will happen for you or any of us. One thing is certain: each of us is special and unique. No one and nothing can take that away.

I hope you see the specialness about you after reading this book. I hope that you are able to view your life in a new light. Take the time to appreciate all your experiences, both those you judge as negative and those you see as positive. Your experiences are part of who you are. In most cases the painful ones are the most important. Learning to transform your negative experiences into something positive is a very empowering skill. Give your self a lot of praise for the work/play you have completed with this book, and in your past. The progress you have made, big or small, shows you have taken risks and that you are courageous.

There is joy to be found in your life. Some joy is subtle and you have to look for it, so pay attention. One way to discover more joy in your life, and the people's lives around you, is to celebrate yourself and them on a daily basis. Celebrations do not have to be big or extravagant. They can be as simple as having a quiet cup of coffee or tea, taking a walk, smiling at yourself in the mirror, or going to the park and swinging like the joyful child that lives within you.

There is only one you and the world wouldn't be as great a place if you were not with us. I wish you joy, excitement, and companionship on you continuing journey.

*"You gain strength, courage and confidence by every experience in which you really stop to look fear in the face. You are able to say to yourself, 'I have lived through this horror. I can take the next thing that comes along.' You must do the thing you think you cannot do."*
Eleanor Roosevelt

## Your thoughts or drawings

*"Let the world know you as you are, not as you think you should be-because sooner or later, if you're posing, you will forget the pose and then where are you?"*
Fanny Brice

*"The road to success is always under construction."*
Lily Tomlin

*"Happiness lies in good health and a bad memory."*
Ingrid Bergman

# Author Biography

Nancy Scheibe has a BA in Communications and Counseling Psychology. She is a nationally known artist, author, workshop facilitator, humorist, actress, and clown. Nancy began focusing on art as a healing tool while using it to recover from an abusive relationship. She has applied these principles while working in volunteer positions with women in shelters and other women's organizations. Nancy has also worked with women in recovery as a Chemical Dependency Counselor. She lives in Ely, Minnesota with her husband.

## Choices Bracelet

*Wear it as a reminder that LOVE is always a choice in your life.*

This bracelet was created out of my need to have a reminder that I always have a choice about how I handle any situation. Our approach to life can be one of love or one of fear – it is a moment-to-moment choice. For many, choosing fear is a habit. We forget we are constantly making choices and that love is always an option. When you feel fear, take a deep breath, and ask yourself ***"What would Love do now?"*** Be gentle with yourself as you strive to change old habits.

Photo features cultured pearl as main stone.

The bracelet is designed with either a **cultured pearl** or an **amethyst** in the center which represents God, your Higher Power, the Great Spirit, or however you name the Divine.

The remainder of the bracelet has alternating white and black beads.

The white beads are **mother of pearl** which represent the love that is always available to each of us at any time.

The black beads are **black onyx** which represent the fear we imagine controls us.

There are more white beads than black—more love than fear.

See page 87 for information on ordering a bracelet.

The **sterling silver** clasp is heart shaped to represent how love holds everything together.

Price
$17.95

# Order Form

For more information or to order
Women's Experience Coloring Books or to purchase a Choices Bracelet contact:

## Creative Journeys
**1764 North Highway 21**
**Ely, MN 55731**

Check or money order must accompany the order.
**Please make your check out to Creative Journeys**

**Ship to:**

Name _____

Address _____

_____

City _____ State _____ Zip _____

Day time phone _____

Evening phone _____

E-mail address _____

---

**Bracelet Orders Only**

**Choice of main bead– check one**

☐ Amethyst (purple)

☐ Cultured Pearl
   (iridescent silver/purple)

**Size—check one**

☐ Small      6 1/2 inches

☐ Medium   7 inches

☐ Large      7 1/2 inches

---

| Item | Quantity | Price Each | Total Price |
|------|----------|-----------|-------------|
| Women's Experience Coloring Book | | 14.95 | |
| Choices Bracelet | | 17.95 | |
| | | Subtotal | |
| | | 6.5% Tax (MN residents only) | |
| | | Shipping and Handling | |
| | | **Total Due** | |

---

### Shipping and Handling (USA)

| | | |
|---|---|---|
| Books | First Book | $2.50 |
| | Each Additional | $1.00 |
| Bracelets | First Bracelet | $2.00 |
| | Each Additional | $ .75 |

When purchasing a book and a bracelet use the price of the
"additional" bracelet to compute shipping and handling
(Book shipping $2.50 + "additional" bracelet $.75 = $3.25)

**Please allow 4 weeks for delivery.**
**Quantity discounts available—**
**write for more information.**

**creativejourneys@2z.net**

87